A BUSH CHRISTENING

ILLUSTRATIONS © Quentin Hole 1976
First published 1976 by
Williams Collins Publishers Pty Ltd, Sydney
First published in this edition 1977
Type set by Filmset Centre, Brisbane
Printed by Dai Nippon Printing Co. (Hong Kong) Ltd.
ISBN 0 00 661222 9

National Library of Australia
Cataloguing in Publication data
Paterson Andrew Barton, 1865-1941,
A bush christening,
For children,
I. Hole, Quentin, illus. II. Title.
AB21 2

A BUSH CHRISTENING

Poem by
A.B. Paterson

Illustrations by
Quentin Hole

Collins SYDNEY · LONDON

On the outer Barcoo where the churches are few,
And men of religion are scanty,
On a road never cross'd 'cept by folk that are lost
One Michael Magee had a shanty.

Now this Mike was the dad of a ten-year-old lad,
Plump, healthy, and stoutly conditioned;
He was strong as the best, but poor Mike had no rest
For the youngster had never been christened.

And his wife used to cry, "If the darlin' should die
Saint Peter would not recognize him."

But by luck he survived till a preacher arrived,

Who agreed straightaway to baptize him.

Now the artful young rogue, while they held their collogue,
With his ear to the keyhole was listenin';
And he muttered in fright, while his features turned white,
"What the divil and all is this christenin'?"

He was none of your dolts—he had seen them brand colts,
And it seemed to his small understanding,
If the man in the frock made him one of the flock
It must mean something very like branding.

So away with a rush he set off for the bush,
While the tears in his eyelids they glistened—
" 'Tis outrageous," says he, "to brand youngsters like me;
I'll be dashed if I'll stop to be christened!"

Like a young native dog he ran into a log,
And his father with language uncivil,
Never heeding the "praste", cried aloud in his haste
"Come out and be christened, you divil!"

But he lay there as snug as a bug in a rug,
And his parents in vain might reprove him,
Till His Reverence spoke (he was fond of a joke)
"I've a notion," says he, "that'll move him."

"Poke a stick up the log, give the spalpeen a prog;
Poke him aisy—don't hurt him or maim him;
'Tis not long that he'll stand, I've the water at hand,

"As he rushes out this end I'll name him.

"Here he comes, and for shame! ye've forgotten the name—
Is it Patsy or Michael or Dinnis?"
Here the youngster ran out, and the priest give a shout—
"Take your chance, anyhow, wid 'Maginnis'!"

As the howling young cub ran away to the scrub
Where he knew that pursuit would be risky,
The priest, as he fled, flung a flask at his head
That was labelled . . .

'MAGINNIS'S WHISKY!'

And Maginnis Magee has been made a J.P.,
And the one thing he hates more than sin is
To be asked by the folk, who have heard of the joke,
How he came to be christened Maginnis!